TERP TIME!

Maryland's Unforgettable National Championship Season

TRIUMPH
BOOKS
CHICAGO

Photo Credits

Allsport: 1.

AP/Wide World Photo: Front Cover, Back Cover, 2-3, 4-all, 5-all, 6-all, 7-all, 9, 10-11, 13, 14-15, 16, 18, 20-21, 22-23, 24, 26, 28, 29, 30-31, 33, 34-35, 36, 36-37, 38, 39, 40, 40-41, 42, 44, 45, 46-47, 48-both, 49, 50, 51, 53, 54-55, 56, 57-both, 58, 59, 60, 61, 62-63, 64, 65, 66, 68, 69, 71, 72-all, 73-all, 74, 77, 79.

Cover and book design: Chris Kozlowski, Dallas, Tex.
Published by: Epic Sports Classics, Birmingham, Ala.

The ACC Tournament

NCAA Tournament

Atlantic Coast Conference Tournament

Terps Race Past FSU in ACC Quarterfinals

Juan Dixon scores 20 points and Byron Mouton adds 18

BY JENNA FRYER
The Associated Press

CHARLOTTE, N.C. — Chris Wilcox was the first to admit he played poorly. Luckily for second-ranked Maryland, plenty of his teammates stepped up.

The Terrapins turned to their reserves for a much-needed second-half spark tonight and pulled away to beat Florida State, 85-59, in the Atlantic Coast Conference tournament quarterfinals.

"I had a terrible game, I just stunk out there," said Wilcox, who averages 11.9 points and 7.6 rebounds but finished with just four points and eight boards Friday.

The Terrapins (26-3) squandered a 12-point lead at the start of the second half to let eighth-seeded Florida State (12-17) briefly make it an uncomfortably close game.

Wilcox was benched during a timeout. Holden replaced him and teamed with Randle to give Maryland energy during a 21-0 second-half run that put the Seminoles away.

"For whatever reason, it took us a long time to get moving," Maryland coach Gary Williams said.

Maryland, the outright ACC regular-season champions for the first time since 1980, moved into the tournament semifinals for the eighth straight year. Tomorrow, the Terrapins face the winner of Virginia-North Carolina State.

Juan Dixon scored 20 points, and Byron Mouton added 18 to lead Maryland, but all the praise went to Holden, who had four points in 15 minutes, and Randle, who added six points in 11 minutes.

Score by Periods	1st	2nd		Total
Florida State	28	31	—	59
Maryland	40	45	—	85

Monte Cummings scored 19 to lead Florida State, which might have played its final game under coach Steve Robinson, who dropped to 64-86 in five seasons with the Seminoles.

Robinson said he planned to meet with Florida State athletic director Dave Hart next week. The coach wouldn't speculate on his future.

The Seminoles, who needed overtime to beat Clemson 91-84 in tonight's opening game, tired late and shot just 30 percent against Maryland while committing 19 turnovers.

Maryland looked in control of things early and took a 40-28 lead into halftime.

But Cummings scored 10 straight points to pull the Seminoles back and Florida State cut it to 42-41 when Trevor Harvey scored on a driving basket and was fouled.

After Harvey made the free throw, Williams called a timeout and benched Wilcox, who had just two points and five rebounds at the time and had thrown the ball away and missed a layup during Florida State's rally.

Holden came in and Maryland's defense improved after the timeout. The Terps scored 21 unanswered points, forced seven turnovers and held Florida State scoreless for 7:14 in a dominating stretch that put Maryland in control of the

Juan Dixon (3) drives past FSU's Marcell Haywood, top, and Monte Cummings, bottom, in the second half.

Florida State's Nigel Dixon, left, battles with Maryland's Byron Mouton for the ball during the first half at the ACC Men's Basketball Tournament.

Florida State (59)

	min	fg m-a	ft m-a	rb o-t	a	pf	tp
Dixon	22	1-3	0-0	1-2	0	1	3
Waleskowski	19	0-2	0-0	2-5	0	2	0
Dixon	22	5-9	3-6	9-12	0	5	13
Arrington	33	3-13	2-4	0-2	4	3	9
Cummings	31	6-12	7-8	2-2	2	2	19
Joiner	18	0-6	0-0	0-2	1	2	0
Bracy	9	0-3	0-0	0-0	0	1	0
Harvey	15	1-5	5-5	3-3	0	1	7
Haywood	7	0-0	0-0	0-1	0	0	0
Mathews	1	0-0	0-0	0-0	0	2	0
Krieg	2	0-1	0-0	0-0	0	0	0
Anderson	2	0-0	0-0	0-0	0	0	0
Richardson	18	2-6	4-4	1-6	0	1	8
Moran	1	0-0	0-0	0-0	0	0	0
Totals	**200**	**18-60**	**21-27**	**18-35**	**7**	**20**	**59**

Percentages: FG-.300, FT-.778. **3-Point Goals:** 2-11, .182 (Dixon 1-2, Arrington 1-6, Joiner 0-2, Bracy 0-1). **Team Rebounds:** 4. **Blocked Shots:** 3 (Dixon, Harvey, A Richardson). **Turnovers:** 19 (Dixon 8, Joiner 3, Bracy 2, Cummings 2, Dixon, Haywood, Waleskowski, Richardson). **Steals:** 9 (Dixon 3, Arrington 2, Waleskowski 2, Cummings, Richardson).

Maryland (85)

	min	fg m-a	ft m-a	rb o-t	a	pf	tp
Mouton	31	5-9	8-8	6-7	2	2	18
Wilcox	27	1-7	2-2	2-8	0	2	4
Baxter	27	4-9	2-3	1-3	2	3	10
Blake	31	4-6	0-0	1-5	7	1	10
Dixon	29	7-14	3-4	2-5	4	4	20
Mccall	4	1-1	0-0	1-2	0	1	2
Collins	5	3-3	2-2	0-1	1	0	8
Nicholas	18	1-4	1-1	0-1	2	1	3
Grinnon	2	0-0	0-0	0-0	0	0	0
Randle	11	2-4	2-2	1-2	0	3	6
Holden	15	2-5	0-0	1-1	1	2	4
Totals	**200**	**30-62**	**20-22**	**15-35**	**19**	**19**	**85**

Percentages: FG-.484, FT-.909. **3-Point Goals:** 5-15, .333 (Mouton 0-1, Blake 2-4, Dixon 3-6, Nicholas 0-3, Holden 0-1). **Team Rebounds:** 5. **Blocked Shots:** 6 (Randle 3, Baxter 2, Dixon). **Turnovers:** 14 (Blake 4, Dixon 3, Baxter 2, Wilcox 2, Nicholas, Collins, Randle). **Steals:** 11 (Blake 5, Baxter 3, Dixon 2, Collins). **Technical fouls:** Florida State 1 (Bench). Maryland 1 (Mouton). **Attendance:** 23,895.

No. 2 Terps Fall in ACC Semifinal to N.C. State

Steve Blake led Maryland with 21 points and 11 assists

By DAVID DROSCHAK
The Associated Press

Score by Periods	1st	2nd		Total
N. Carolina State	40	46	—	86
Maryland	38	44	—	82

CHARLOTTE, N.C. — Maryland coach Gary Williams has gotten used to losing in the Atlantic Coast Conference tournament.

The second-ranked Terrapins last captured the ACC tourney 18 years ago and were riding a 13-game winning streak before today's 86-82 loss to North Carolina State in the semifinals.

"I remember this feeling," Williams said. "It's funny, it didn't take long to remember it."

Anthony Grundy scored 24 points, and Julius Hodge sank a big 3-pointer with 1:17 left to key the Wolfpack upset. N.C. State, which snapped a six-game skid against Maryland, shot 65 percent in the second half and made 11 3-pointers one day after hitting 13.

"A good team doesn't like to get beat, so they came out and gave us their best shot," Williams said.

Regular-season ACC champion Maryland (26-4) was in its eighth straight conference semifinal, but it has advanced to the title game just once in that span under Williams — in 2000, when it lost to Duke.

"We took everybody's shot during the regular season and did what we had to do to win the regular season," Williams said.

"We knew we would have to come down here and play really well. It just didn't look like we were

Chris Wilcox, center, shoots between North Carolina State defenders Anthony Grundy, left, and Marcus Melvin (54) in the first half.

as sharp as we were last week — and mentally it's been a long haul. Hopefully, we can get that mental edge back."

N.C. State (22-9) used a unique game plan to reach the tourney final for the first time since 1997, when Herb Sendek became the first coach to take an eighth-seeded team to the championship game. The Wolfpack lost the title to North Carolina that year.

As Illian Evtimov intercepted a pass at the buzzer, Sendek threw his arms up and his players mobbed each other at center court.

"We've been hungry all year," Grundy said. "We just didn't want to come out here and let them have their way with us. We got into the game, we got up and that gave us more confidence. We felt we were able to play with them."

The fourth-seeded Wolfpack won by pressuring Maryland guard Steve Blake with a fullcourt trapping press. When the Terrapins pounded the ball down low to Lonny Baxter or Chris Wilcox, N.C. State surrounded them with as many as four players at a time.

"We changed defenses a lot, and our big guys stepped up," Grundy said. "We just got great help."

It also helped that Maryland star Juan Dixon had an off-game, going 6-of-16 for just 13 points.

Dixon has more than 2,100 career points, but will leave Maryland without an ACC tournament title.

"Those guys were prepared and they outplayed us on both ends of the floor," Dixon said. "That's why in these tournaments you've got to be ready to

NC State's Marcus Melvin (54) battles for a rebound with Lonny Baxter.

play for 40 minutes. If not, you can lose just like that and be gone."

The Terrapins are still expected to be a No. 1 seed in the NCAA tournament.

"Maybe this is good for us," Dixon said. "This brings us down off that high."

Grundy was coming off a career-high 32-point effort in a 20-point quarterfinal win over Virginia — and he was just as spectacular in this one, until missing some important free throws late.

The senior guard was 9-of-12 from the field with eight rebounds. Marcus Melvin added 19 points, Archie Miller 16.

Blake led Maryland with 21 points and 11 assists.

The Wolfpack went up, 67-64, with 7:13 left before going on a 10-0 run to break the game open — or so it appeared. Miller had a 3-pointer and two free throws in the spurt, while Grundy had a twisting layup and Melvin a 3-pointer.

However, the Terrapins didn't go quietly.

Three free throws by Blake got Maryland to 81-78 before Hodge hit his 3-pointer.

But poor free-throw shooting by the ACC's best team from the line kept Maryland in it until the end.

The Terrapins had a chance to tie it twice in the final 30 seconds, but Dixon threw the ball away once and his off-balance 28-footer with 3.2 seconds wasn't close.

Grundy sealed it with a free throw.

N.C. State started 9-for-15 as Melvin made three 3-pointers in a span of five minutes and the Wolfpack bolted to a 24-12 lead.

After Melvin's layup put the Wolfpack up by 12, Williams called his second 30-second timeout to try to slow down N.C. State's surge.

Coming out of the huddle, Williams stomped his foot on the floor in vintage Lefty Driesell fashion and yelled: "Come on, wake up!"

The Terrapins responded. Williams inserted Tahj Holden into the frontcourt in place of the slumping Wilcox for the second straight game, and Maryland scored 11 consecutive points as part of a 19-2 run.

But N.C. State settled down and got a layup and 3-pointer from Grundy over the final 1:44 of the half to take a two-point lead at the break.

NC State (86)

	min	fg m-a	ft m-a	rb o-t	a	pf	tp
Hodge	29	6-8	1-3	0-1	5	4	14
Powell	32	0-1	0-0	1-2	0	0	0
Melvin	37	7-12	1-4	1-6	3	3	19
Grundy	37	9-12	4-7	1-8	4	3	24
Miller	36	3-7	7-8	1-4	3	4	16
Evtimov	30	4-7	3-4	0-2	5	4	12
Sherrill	6	0-2	0-0	0-1	0	0	0
Crawford	12	0-0	1-2	0-2	2	2	1
Collins	10	0-0	0-0	1-1	0	0	0
TEAM				1			
Totals	**200**	**29-49**	**17-28**	**5-28**	**22**	**20**	**86**

Percentages: FG .592, FT .607. **3-Point Goals:** 11-27, .407 (Melvin 4-8, Miller 3-7, Grundy 2-4, Hodge 1-2, Evtimov 1-4, Sherrill 0-2). **Team Rebounds:** 5. **Blocked Shots:** 0. **Turnovers:** 18 (Grundy 7, Melvin 5, Crawford 2, Collins 1, Sherrill 1, Miller 1, TEAM 1). **Steals:** 7 (Hodge 3, Miller 2, Grundy 1, Emtimov 1). **Technical Fouls:** 0.

Maryland (82)

	min	fg m-a	ft m-a	rb o-t	a	pf	tp
Mouton	25	1-5	7-8	3-7	3	3	9
Wilcox	24	6-14	3-4	1-3	2	2	15
Baxter	32	6-9	3-3	3-7	0	5	15
Dixon	39	6-16	0-0	1-3	2	4	13
Blake	38	7-9	5-6	0-5	11	3	21
Nicholas	19	2-5	2-2	1-2	1	2	7
Randle	8	0-1	0-0	0-1	0	0	0
Holden	15	1-2	0-0	1-2	1	3	2
Totals	**200**	**29-61**	**20-23**	**10-30**	**20**	**22**	**82**

Percentages: FG .475, FT .870. **3-Point Goals:** 4-14, .286 (Blake 2-4, Dixon 1-4, Nicholas 1-4). **Team Rebounds:** 1. **Blocked Shots:** 2 (Wilcox 1, Randle 1). **Turnovers:** 13 (Blake 4, Baxter 3, Dixon 2, Holden 2, Wilcox 1, Mouton 1). **Steals:** 11 (Blake 6, Mouton 2, Wilcox 1, Baxter 1, Holden 1). **Technical Fouls:** 1 (Holden). **Attendance:** 23,895.

NCAA
Tournament

Terps Roll Past Siena in NCAA Tourney Round 1

Juan Dixon scores 29 points against the Saints

BY DAVID GINSBURG
The Associated Press

WASHINGTON — Juan Dixon is leaving nothing to chance in his final NCAA tournament.

A determined Dixon scored 29 points Friday night as top-seeded Maryland cruised past Siena 85-70 in a first-round East Regional game.

Dixon, a senior guard, knows that his next loss will be his last as a college player. So he's not going to stop hustling on the court until the final buzzer of his final game.

"I just wanted to come out and be aggressive," said Dixon, who shot 10-for-17 from the field and made all four free throws. "This is my last time going through this, and I want to tell myself that I went out being aggressive."

Dixon drove to the basket, pulled up for jumpers and deftly passed to open teammates when Siena double-teamed him.

"Once he gets his confidence, he can't be stopped," Maryland forward Byron Mouton said. "I told him to keep shooting, because he was making them. His shooting was a big difference in the game."

Dixon, who scored 20 in the first half, fell two points short of matching the school record shared for points in an NCAA tournament game, held jointly by Len Bias and Joe Smith.

The fourth-ranked Terrapins (27-4) on Sunday will face eighth-seeded Wisconsin, which advanced by defeating St. John's 80-70 earlier Friday night.

Playing against the only team in the 65-team field with a losing record, Maryland made itself right at home at the MCI Center, which is only 20 minutes from the College Park campus.

Score by Periods	1st	2nd		Total
Siena College	**38**	**32**	—	**70**
Maryland	**52**	**33**	—	**85**

The Terrapins have played two games a year at the arena in each of the past five seasons. Their familiarity with the building served them well, as did the backing of the hometown crowd.

"We've got the homecourt advantage," Mouton said. "The crowd gave us the extra boost we needed."

Maryland probably would have won without those factors working in its favor. The Terrapins were eager to bounce back from Saturday's loss to North Carolina State in the Atlantic Coast Conference tournament, and Siena had the misfortune of being Maryland's next opponent.

The loss ended an improbable run by the Saints (17-19), 12-18 before winning the Metro Atlantic Athletic Conference tournament and beating Alcorn State, 81-77, in an opening-round game Tuesday.

That victory enabled Siena to become only the second team with a losing record to win an NCAA tournament game. But the Saints' bid to become the first 16th seed to beat a No. 1 seed was abruptly rejected by a Maryland team on a mission to win its first national championship.

Siena had 16 turnovers, shot 41 percent and was only 8-for-22 from 3-point range.

"They're good enough without our help, and we

Juan Dixon (3) moves inside against Siena's Prosper Karangwa, left, Dwayne Archbold, rear, and Tommy Mitchell (25) in the first half.

Byron Mouton (1) grabs a rebound over Siena's James Clinton, left, Prosper Karangwa, center, and Dwayne Archbold (24) in the first half.

"You always feel pressure. What do you say if you lose a game like that, and the No. 1 seed? 'I'm going to Mexico?' You don't say I'm going to Disneyland, I know that."
— **Coach Gary Williams**

helped them quite a bit," Saints coach Rob Lanier said.

James Clinton scored 16 points and Dwayne Archbold added 14 for Siena. Prosper Karangwa, who scored a career-high 31 against Alcorn State, was held to 7 on 3-for-8 shooting.

"They're real good," Archbold said. "We made a lot of mistakes, and they capitalized on almost every one of them."

Siena trailed, 24-21, before the Terrapins used a layup by Lonny Baxter, an alley-oop dunk by Chris Wilcox and a four-point play by reserve Drew Nicholas to go up by 11.

The Saints hung around a little longer, but they never could come up with a way to control Dixon, who easily thwarted Siena's man-to-man defense and its 2-3 zone.

Dixon single-handedly turned a 10-point cushion into a 50-31 lead during a 3-minute stretch of the first half. First, he made two free throws and hit a 3-pointer. He then drove to the basket and passed to Tahj Holden, who was fouled on a dunk and made the free throw.

Clifton stopped the run with a basket, but Dixon answered with a 3-pointer.

Maryland led, 52-38, at halftime, but Coach Gary Williams angrily called a timeout early in the second half after Siena closed to 52-42. Dixon then scored six points in an 8-0 burst that made it 60-42, ending all suspense except whether the ACC player of the year would break the school single-game scoring mark.

He didn't make it, but it was still a very good night for the Terrapins.

Sienna (70)

	min	fg m-a	ft m-a	rb o-t	a	pf	tp
Cavo	26	6-11	0-0	3-3	2	4	13
Clinton	31	6-10	2-2	3-4	2	2	16
Miller	25	0-1	2-2	1-2	2	3	2
Karangwa	35	3-8	0-0	0-2	6	3	7
Archbold	37	4-18	4-4	0-9	3	4	14
Price	12	3-7	2-2	2-4	1	0	8
Andrews	11	2-3	0-0	1-1	0	1	4
Harvey	0	0-0	0-0	0-0	0	0	0
Mitchell	14	2-4	0-0	0-1	1	0	6
Sniezyk	9	0-2	0-0	0-3	0	0	0
TEAM			1-5				
Totals	**200**	**26-64**	**10-10**	**11-34**	**17**	**17**	**70**

Percentages: FG .406, FT 1.000. **3-Point Goals:** 8-22, .364 (Cavo 1-5, Clinton 2-2, Miller 0-1, Karangwa 1-2, Archbold 2-9, Price 0-1, Mitchell 2-2). **Team Rebounds:** 5. **Blocked Shots:** 3 (Clinton 2, Miller 1). **Turnovers:** 16 (Cavo 1, Clinton 1, Miller 2, Karangwa 4, Archbold 1, Price 2, Andrews 2, Mitchell 2, Sniezyk 1). **Steals:** 9 (Karangwa 4, Archbold 1, Price 3, Mitchell 1). **Technical Fouls:** 0.

Maryland (85)

	min	fg m-a	ft m-a	rb o-t	a	pf	tp
Mouton	29	2-6	2-2	3-4	3	3	6
Wilcox	25	3-8	1-1	1-4	3	2	7
Baxter	27	6-11	2-5	1-9	0	1	14
Dixon	32	10-17	4-4	0-2	4	2	29
Blake	33	4-9	0-0	1-5	11	2	11
McCall	2	0-0	0-0	0-0	0	1	0
Collins	2	0-0	0-0	0-0	0	0	0
Nicholas	23	3-6	1-1	0-2	2	2	9
Randle	13	2-4	0-0	1-3	1	0	4
Holden	14	2-4	1-1	3-6	1	1	5
TEAM			1-2				
Totals	**200**	**32-65**	**11-14**	**12-39**	**25**	**14**	**85**

Percentages: FG .492, FT .786. **3-Point Goals:** 10-22, .455 (Dixon 5-8, Blake 3-7, Nicholas 2-4, Holden 0-1, Wilcox 0-1, Mouton 0-1). **Team Rebounds:** 2. **Blocked Shots:** 5 (Baxter 3, Blake 1, Holden 1). **Turnovers:** 25 (Mouton 3, Blake 3, Nicholas 3, Wilcox 2, Baxter 2, Dixon 2, Collins 1). **Steals:** 8 (Wilcox 3, Blake 2, Mouton 1, Dixon 1, Randle 1). **Technical Fouls:** 0. **Attendance.:** 18,770.

Maryland Cruises Past Wisconsin in 2nd Round

Juan Dixon breaks a pair of school scoring records

BY DAVID GINSBURG
The Associated Press

Score by Periods	1st	2nd		Total
Wisconsin	30	27	—	57
Maryland	38	49	—	87

WASHINGTON — Juan Dixon stepped into the Maryland record book, and the top-seeded Terrapins methodically marched into the NCAA tournament's final 16 for the sixth time in nine years.

Dixon scored 29 points to break two school scoring records, leading Maryland past eighth-seeded Wisconsin, 87-57, today in the second round of the East Regional.

Chris Wilcox had 18 points for Maryland (28-4), which will next face fourth-seeded Kentucky on Friday in Syracuse. The Terrapins, who have won 15 of 16 since Jan. 17, matched the 1998-99 team for most wins in a season and set a school mark for margin of victory in an NCAA tournament game.

Dixon, a senior guard, broke Len Bias' team record for career points and also eclipsed Bias' mark for career points in the NCAA tournament. Dixon has 2,172 points overall and 197 in his four trips to the tourney.

Dixon was 10-for-19 from the field, including 4-for-7 from 3-point range, and 5-of-6 on free throws — a suitable encore to his 29-point performance against Siena in the tournament opener.

Wisconsin (19-13), which tied for the Big Ten

Maryland's Chris Wilcox (54) dunks over Wisconsin's Travon Davis, center, during the second half of their NCAA East Regional second-round game in Washington, D.C.

regular-season title, closed its first season under Coach Bo Ryan by losing two of three. The Badgers were seeking to duplicate their tournament run of two years ago, when they advanced to the Final Four after defeating No. 1-seeded Arizona in the second round.

Charlie Wills scored 17 points for Wisconsin, which absorbed its worst beating in 18 NCAA tournament games.

The Badgers had no answers for Dixon or a defense that caused them to miss 28 of their first 40 shots while Maryland built a 60-35 lead.

Up 38-30 at halftime, the Terrapins opened the second half with a 22-5 run to thrill the sell-out crowd at the MCI Center, which was filled predominantly with Terrapins fans.

Dixon scored 15 points in the run, including a pair of 3-pointers and a layup off a steal.

The game was tied five times in the opening 13 minutes before Maryland used its inside-outside attack to take control.

After Lonny Baxter and Wilcox scored in the lane to make it 23-all, Drew Nicholas and Steve Blake hit successive 3-pointers to put Maryland ahead for good.

Wills stopped the 10-point run with a layup before Dixon topped Bias' record with a 3-pointer for a 32-25 lead. Minutes later, Dixon hit a jumper and added two free throws to cap a 19-5 spree and put the Terrapins up by 10.

Above: Juan Dixon (3) shoots over Wisconsin's Kirk Penney (20) and Devin Harris. Left: Dixon battles with the Badgers' Freddie Owens (24) and Kirk Penney, background, in the first half.

Wisconsin's Travon Davis (2) tries to escape from Juan Dixon in the second half.

Wisconsin (57)

	min	fg m-a	ft m-a	rb o-t	a	pf	tp
Harris	30	3-9	0-0	0-1	0	2	7
Wills	29	6-12	3-6	2-6	1	3	17
Mader	25	1-6	0-0	4-8	4	3	2
Davis	34	5-7	4-5	1-4	3	2	15
Penney	37	3-14	3-3	1-4	1	0	9
Hanson	3	0-2	0-0	0-0	0	2	0
Owens	15	0-4	0-0	0-1	0	3	0
Wilkinson	27	3-5	0-0	1-4	2	4	7
TOTALS	**200**	**21-59**	**10-14**	**9-28**	**11**	**19**	**57**

Percentages: FG-.356, FT-.714. **3-Point Goals:** 5-19, .263 (Harris 1-4, Wills 2-4, Davis 1-1, Penney 0-6, Hanson 0-1, Owens 0-1, Wilkinson 1-2). **Team Rebounds:** 4. Blocked Shots: 4 (Mader 2, Harris 2). **Turnovers:** 14 (Harris 3, Davis 2, Mader 2, Owens 2, Wills 2, Penney 2, Wilkinson). **Steals:** 6 (Penney 2, Wilkinson 2, Owens 1, Wills 1).

Maryland (87)

	min	fg m-a	ft m-a	rb o-t	a	pf	tp
Mouton	25	0-4	2-2	3-7	1	1	2
Wilcox	26	9-13	0-1	1-7	1	0	18
Baxter	28	5-6	6-7	1-7	3	3	16
Dixon	36	10-19	5-6	3-5	3	1	29
Blake	30	1-4	0-0	0-2	4	3	3
Badu	2	0-0	0-0	0-0	2	0	0
Mccall	5	0-0	0-0	0-0	0	0	0
Collins	3	1-2	0-0	0-0	0	0	2
Nicholas	20	3-7	0-0	0-2	2	1	8
Grinnon	2	0-1	0-0	2-2	0	0	0
Randle	10	2-4	0-0	2-4	0	3	4
Holden	13	1-2	2-2	1-1	1	2	5
TOTALS	**200**	**32-62**	**15-18**	**13-37**	**17**	**14**	**87**

Percentages: FG-.516, FT-.833. **3-Point Goals:** 8-16, .500 (Dixon 4-7, Blake 1-3, Nicholas 2-4, Holden 1-2). **Team Rebounds:** 4. **Blocked Shots:** 5 (Baxter 4, Wilcox). **Turnovers:** 10 (Mouton 3, Baxter, Blake, Wilcox, Randle, Badu, Dixon, Holden). **Steals:** 9 (Baxter 2, Dixon 2, Blake, Mouton, Nicholas, Wilcox, Collins). **Technical fouls:** None. **Attendance:** 18,789.

Terps Romp Past UK to Reach Elite 8 Round

Juan Dixon scores 19 points against the Wildcats

BY JIM O'CONNELL
The Associated Press

Score by Periods	1st	2nd		Total
Kentucky	**33**	**35**	**—**	**68**
Maryland	**39**	**39**	**—**	**78**

SYRACUSE, N.Y. — No jumping around, no excited hugs, no pointing to the stands.

Maryland's players simply shook hands with the team they beat and walked off the court, closer to a second straight Final Four.

"They're a veteran team. Sometimes I wish they had more emotion," Terrapins coach Gary Williams said. "We are not surprised when we win. We go in thinking we're good enough to win and when we do, we move on to the next game."

Despite a quiet second half from All-American Juan Dixon, top-seeded Maryland just moved right along tonight, beating Kentucky, 78-68, in the East Regional semifinals.

Maryland (29-4) will play second-seeded Connecticut in Sunday's regional final.

The teams met in Washington on Dec. 3, with the Terrapins winning, 77-65. The stakes are a lot higher this time, with Maryland looking to get to the Final Four for the second time in school history. Connecticut, which beat Southern Illinois, 71-59, today, has also been to the Final Four just once, when the Huskies won it all in 1999.

The Huskies are "one of those teams that always gets better," Williams said.

"It's two different teams now, but we're a better team also."

Dixon, the Atlantic Coast Conference player of the year, had only four points over the final 14 minutes of the Terrapins' win over Kentucky. He didn't have to score, though.

Unlike in the Terrapins' first two wins in the tournament — when the senior guard poured in 29 points each time — Dixon didn't dominate the scoring column.

"Today I didn't have to score 29. I only needed to score 19 and make some defensive plays," said Dixon, who was 6-for-15 from the field and had seven rebounds and four assists.

"Hopefully we can keep this up."

Maryland's 16th victory in 17 games ended the up-and-down season of fifth-seeded Kentucky (22-10), which got only 17 points from senior star Tayshaun Prince — 24 fewer than he scored in a second-round victory over Tulsa.

"Prince is going to get his looks. We just wanted to make sure he didn't get a lot of open looks," Williams said. "Byron Mouton did a good job on him, and we tried to help off the screen and convince him he wasn't open."

Prince, who was 19-for-35 from the field in the first two tournament games, was 6-for-16 against the Terrapins.

"I had plenty of opportunities and didn't get it down," he said. "They did a pretty good job of playing defense. Others double-teamed me more. They were straight up until I had the opportunity to shoot."

Both Maryland and Kentucky played solid defense, and neither came within seven points of its season scoring average.

Juan Dixon goes to the basket as Kentucky's Marquis Estill (50) defends during the second half.

Right: Kentucky's Tayshaun Prince soars over Juan Dixon in the first half during the NCAA East Regional semifinal at the Carrier Dome in Syracuse, N.Y.

Drew Nicholas' 3-pointer with 9:54 left gave Maryland the lead for good at 56-53, but the Wildcats wouldn't let the Terrapins pull away.

Marquis Estill made two free throws with 5:05 to play to get Kentucky within 66-63, but Chris Wilcox and Lonny Baxter each made two for Maryland to make it 70-63.

The Wildcats' Chuck Hayes scored with 1:53 left to make it a five-point game. Dixon had four free throws, and Mouton added two more to give Maryland its late cushion.

Baxter had 16 points for Maryland, while Wilcox had 15 and Mouton 14. Keith Bogans scored 15 for Kentucky, and Estill had 12.

Maryland is in the regional finals for the fourth time, the others coming in 1973, '75, and last year, when it lost to eventual champion Duke in the national semifinals.

"I was impressed with their composure down the stretch and making their free throws," Kentucky coach Tubby Smith said. "It's a sign of a poised, mature, veteran team."

Kentucky fought through a season of distractions that included players transferring and being suspended, injuries and the usual high expectations of one of the nation's most high-profile programs. The Wildcats went to a regional final every year from 1995-99 — winning NCAA championships in 1996 and '98 — but have not been back since.

"I was impressed with their composure down the stretch and making their free throws. It's a sign of a poised, mature, veteran team."

— Kentucky coach Tubby Smith

Kentucky (68)

	min	fg m-a	ft m-a	rb o-t	a	pf	tp
Prince	38	6-15	2-2	1-7	2	2	17
Hayes	23	3-6	1-2	2-7	1	1	7
Camara	27	4-11	2-4	4-8	1	3	10
Bogans	28	6-14	1-3	1-2	2	3	15
Hawkins	35	2-8	0-0	0-5	7	3	6
Carruth	5	0-1	0-0	0-0	0	1	0
Blevins	5	0-0	0-0	0-0	0	0	0
Fitch	13	0-2	0-0	0-0	0	0	0
Daniels	7	0-1	1-2	0-1	0	2	1
Estill	19	4-4	4-4	0-2	0	5	12
TOTALS	**200**	**25-62**	**11-17**	**8-32**	**13**	**20**	**68**

Percentages: FG-.403, FT-.647. **3-Point Goals:**
7-19, .368 (Prince 3-7, Hayes 0-1, Camara 0-1,
Bogans 2-6, Hawkins 2-3, Fitch 0-1). **Team
Rebounds:** 5. **Blocked Shots:** 4 (Camara 2,
Estill, Fitch). **Turnovers:** 14 (Hawkins 4, Camara
3, Prince 3, Daniels 2, Bogans, Estill). **Steals:** 8
(Bogans 2, Camara 2, Hawkins 2, Prince, Hayes).

Maryland (78)

	min	fg m-a	ft m-a	rb o-t	a	pf	tp
Mouton	31	5-9	4-5	3-6	2	1	14
Wilcox	30	4-10	7-8	0-2	1	1	15
Baxter	30	6-9	4-4	1-5	0	3	16
Blake	31	2-9	0-1	1-3	5	3	4
Dixon	37	6-15	4-4	1-7	4	2	19
Nicholas	20	3-6	0-0	1-3	5	2	8
Randle	8	0-1	0-0	0-1	0	1	0
Holden	13	0-0	2-2	0-2	0	3	2
TOTALS	**200**	**26-59**	**21-24**	**7-29**	**17**	**16**	**78**

Percentages: FG-.441, FT-.875. **3-Point Goals:**
5-16, .313 (Wilcox 0-1, Blake 0-3, Dixon 3-8,
Nicholas 2-4). **Team Rebounds:** 7. **Blocked
Shots:** 1 (Holden). **Turnovers:** 14 (Blake 4,
Baxter 2, Dixon 2, Nicholas 2, Wilcox 2, Holden,
Mouton). **Steals:** 7 (Blake 2, Dixon, Holden,
Mouton, Nicholas, Wilcox). **Technical fouls:**
None. **Attendance:** 29,633.

Above: Chris Wilcox reacts after a slam dunk against Kentucky's Jules Camara, right, and Tayshaun Prince (21) as Byron Mouton, foreground, looks on.

Right: Maryland's Chris Wilcox goes for a shot as UK's Chuck Hayes (44) defends in the first half.

Kentucky's Marquis Estill (50) and Cliff Hawkins (1) defend against Chris Wilcox (54) during the first half of the NCAA East Regional semifinal.

Maryland's Lonny Baxter (35) goes to the basket over Kentucky's Marquis Estill.

"They're a veteran team. Sometimes I wish they had more emotion. We are not surprised when we win. We go in thinking we're good enough to win and when we do, we move on to the next game."

— Coach Gary Williams

Tayshaun Prince sits dejected on the bench in the closing moments of Kentucky's 78-68 loss to Maryland.

Seniors Lead the Way Back to the Final Four

Lonny Baxter has a season-high 29 points against UConn

By Jim O'Connell
The Associated Press

Syracuse, N.Y. — Back and forth, back and forth — until Steve Blake spoke up and came through.

Pulled from a tight East Regional final because of poor defense, and without a point, the junior guard still wanted a shot.

So when Maryland coach Gary Williams barked instructions to get the ball to All-American Juan Dixon with less than a minute left, Blake cut Williams off and announced he would take care of things.

With 25 second left today and the shot clock nearing zero, Blake sank a 3-pointer for his first bucket of the game, leading top-seeded Maryland to a 90-82 victory over Connecticut and a second straight trip to the Final Four.

"That shot was the biggest one I could hit for this team," said Blake, who missed his only two attempts until then. "At the last timeout, I told the guys to look for me. I was just kind of freelancing. I knew if I hit the shot it would be tough for them. I just got a good look as the shot clock was winding down."

That put Maryland up, 86-80, and was the clinching blow in a tremendous display of basket-for-basket play. There were eight ties and seven lead changes in the final 13 minutes.

"It's hard when the game is back and forth like

Maryland's Lonny Baxter (35) puts up a shot as UConn's Mike Hayes, left, and Caron Butler (3) defend during the NCAA East Regional Championship.

Score by Periods	1st	2nd		Total
Connecticut	37	45	—	82
Maryland	44	46	—	90

that," UConn forward Johnnie Selvie said.

"Every time we would get the lead, they always answered, and that's what good teams do. Every time they got the lead, we answered. It was just two very good teams going to war."

Lonny Baxter had a season-high 29 points, and Dixon scored 27 for Maryland (30-4), which reached the 30-victory mark for the first time.

Second-seeded UConn stayed in the game thanks to sophomore Caron Butler, who had 26 of his 32 points during a second half in which neither team lead by more than three points from the 14-minute mark until the final 36 seconds.

"We have tough guys. We didn't think we would lose this game," Williams said.

"We're going back. We want to do something this year."

Maryland, which lost to eventual national champion Duke in last year's Final Four, will play another No. 1 seed, Kansas, on Saturday in Atlanta. The Jayhawks beat Oregon, 104-86, in the Midwest Regional final.

Just as there was no wild on-court celebration after their regional semifinal win over Kentucky, the Terrapins were again matter of fact after beating Connecticut (27-7).

For a while.

Williams arrived at the postgame news conference wearing a Maryland warmup outfit, because his suit and tie were soaked during the postgame celebration.

"Our guys were accused of not being very emotional after Kentucky," Williams said. "They were very emotional in our locker room. That's why I'm wearing this attire."

Maryland scored the final eight points of the first half to take a 44-37 lead — UConn's biggest deficit of the tourney to that juncture — but Butler brought the Huskies back.

"Caron Butler carried that team in the second half, but we stayed strong and focused," Dixon said. "We didn't want this to be our last game. We strapped down on defense when we had to and made free throws."

Baxter, the regional's Most Outstanding Player,

Lonny Baxter (35) tries to get past Connecticut's Emeka Okafor.

was 7-for-12 from the field, 15-for-18 from the free throw line and grabbed nine rebounds. He had 24 points and 10 rebounds in the teams' first meeting this season, a 77-65 Maryland victory on Dec. 3.

"I just stepped up to the line and tried to make every free throw I took," Baxter said. "We just know how to win and we stayed with it to the end."

The Huskies, who had won 12 games in a row, kept this one as close as a game can be.

Butler, who had a career-high 34 points in last Sunday's second-round victory over North Carolina State, only played 13 minutes in the first half because of foul trouble.

He hit his first three 3-point attempts in the second half, the last of which gave the Huskies a 54-53 lead with 13:11 left and set up the wild ending.

"We needed someone else to make a play besides Caron," Connecticut coach Jim Calhoun said. "The kids were standing around watching him, waiting for him to make a play."

Baxter gave Maryland the lead for good with a hook shot that made it 81-79 with 2:08 left.

Connecticut was within 83-80 when Blake became the hero.

The point guard was having a poor game and was banished to the bench by Williams with about 5 minutes remaining.

Maryland took a timeout with 34 seconds left on the game clock and 14 on the shot clock. Blake wound up with the ball and his 3-pointer went through.

After a UConn miss, Blake added two free throws for an 88-80 lead.

Chris Wilcox added 13 points for Maryland, which shot 50.9 percent (27-for-53) from the field and was 31-for-35 on free throws. The Terrapins were the first team this season to shoot better than 50 percent against the Huskies.

A year ago, Maryland made the first Final Four appearance in school history. Now the Terps head back having won 17 of 18 games, the only loss coming to North Carolina State in the Atlantic Coast Conference tournament semifinals.

Right: Byron Mouton, bottom, and UConn's Caron Butler battle for the ball.

Connecticut (82)

	min	fg m-a	ft m-a	rb o-t	a	pf	tp
Butler	33	9-13	11-14	5-7	4	3	32
Selvie	37	2-7	3-4	5-6	1	3	7
Okafor	23	2-5	2-4	0-6	0	4	6
TBrown	34	5-10	0-0	0-2	3	4	12
Robertson	28	5-10	4-4	0-1	1	3	15
Gordon	25	1-7	5-6	0-1	3	0	8
JBrown	10	1-3	0-0	0-2	0	2	2
Hazelton	2	0-0	0-0	0-0	0	0	0
Hayes	7	0-0	0-2	1-1	0	4	0
Tooles	1	0-0	0-0	0-0	0	0	0
Totals	200	25-55	25-34	11-26	12	23	82

Percentages: FG .455, FT .735. **3-Point Goals:**
7-17, .412 (Butler 3-5, T. Brown 2-4, Gordon 1-4,
Robertson 1-4). **Team Rebounds:** 5. **Blocked
Shots:** 5 (J. Brown, Hayes, Okafor, Robertson,
Selvie). **Turnovers:** 14 (Gordon 4, T. Brown 2,
Butler 2, Robertson 2, Selvie 2, J. Brown, Hayes).
Steals: 3 (Robertson 2, Butler). **Technical Fouls:**
None.

Maryland (90)

	min	fg m-a	ft m-a	rb o-t	a	pf	tp
Mouton	34	1-4	2-2	1-3	1	3	4
Wilcox	25	5-10	3-4	2-4	0	4	13
Baxter	36	7-12	15-18	3-9	1	2	29
Dixon	39	10-18	4-4	0-1	3	3	27
Blake	27	1-3	2-2	1-4	6	3	5
McCall	1	0-0	0-0	0-0	0	0	0
Nicholas	20	0-1	2-2	0-2	3	1	2
Randle	4	1-2	0-0	1-1	0	3	2
Holden	14	2-3	3-3	0-2	0	4	8
Totals	200	27-53	31-35	8-26	14	23	90

Percentages: FG .509, FT .886. **3-Point Goals:**
5-9, .556 (Dixon 3-5, Blake 1-1, Holden 1-1,
Mouton 0-1, Nicholas 0-1). **Team Rebounds:** 7.
Blocked Shots: 2 (Baxter, Wilcox). **Turnovers:**
13 (Baxter 4, Dixon 3, Holden 2, Wilcox 2,
Mouton, Nicholas). **Steals:** 7 (Mouton 2, Baxter,
Blake, Dixon, Nicholas, Wilcox). **Technical Fouls:**
None. **Attendance:** 29,252.

Maryland's Ryan Randle enjoys
a dunk against the Huskies
during the NCAA East Regional
Championship at the Carrier
Dome in Syracuse, N.Y.

Right: UConn's Emeka Okafor sits in the lockerroom, reflecting on the Terps 90-82 win.

Below: Coach Gary Williams gets excited during the 2002 NCAA Men's Basketball East Regional against Connecticut.

Lonny Baxter holds a piece of the net during the net-cutting ceremonies following Maryland's 90-82 win over the Huskies.

UConn's Taliek Brown, center, looks for a way out from behind Maryland defenders Juan Dixon, Chris Wilcox, right, and Lonny Baxter, rear.

Terps coach Gary Williams finishes the net-cutting ceremony in the Carrier Dome by throwing the net to members of his team.

Dixon, Terps Earn First Trip to Finals

All-American guard scores 33 points to lead Maryland

By Jim O'Connell
The Associated Press

Score by Periods	1st	2nd		Total
Kansas	37	51	—	88
Maryland	44	53	—	97

ATLANTA — Juan Dixon made darn sure Maryland's return to the Final Four didn't end after one game this time.

With its All-American guard leading the way, the Terrapins reached the national championship game for the first time with a 97-88 victory over Kansas on tonight.

Unlike last season when the Terps blew a 22-point lead to Duke in its first Final Four appearance, Maryland managed to make sure this big lead held up in the matchup of No. 1 seeds.

"It was a strange feeling. When the buzzer went off we were playing for the championship," coach Gary Williams said.

Dixon hit a baseline jumper with 1:14 to play that gave Maryland an 89-82 lead after Kansas had cut a 20-point lead to five. The Jayhawks still weren't done and neither was Dixon, who finished with 33 points.

Kansas hit two 3-pointers in the final 30 seconds. After the first, Dixon made two free throws to make it 92-85. After the second, Kansas called a timeout it didn't have and Dixon made one of two free throws on the technical to make it 93-88 with 19 seconds left. That was as close as the Jayhawks would get.

Maryland (31-4) will play Indiana for the national championship on Monday night. The fifth-seeded Hoosiers (25-11) advanced with a 73-64 victory over second-seeded Oklahoma.

Steve Blake and Juan Dixon embrace after the Terps' victory.

"A lot of people were doubting Indiana, but a lot of people were doubting us," Maryland's Taj Holden said.

Chris Wilcox added 18 points and nine rebounds for Maryland and Steve Blake had eight points and 11 assists.

Now Williams has a chance at his national championship and the Terrapins have an opportunity to erase last season's nightmare. Many of the players said this week they had still not gotten over the 95-84 loss to eventual national champion Duke in Minneapolis.

Williams, who once played for Maryland, celebrated the win with a chest bump with Wilcox.

Nick Collison had 21 points and 10 rebounds for the Jayhawks, while All-American forward Drew Gooden finished with 15 points on 5-for-12 shooting and had nine rebounds.

Things were far from perfect at the start for Maryland, as Kansas (33-4) jumped to a 13-2 lead inside the opening four minutes. Rallying in the first half seemed to fit the Terrapins much better than holding a big lead did a year ago.

Despite center Lonny Baxter being limited to three minutes in the first half because of foul trouble, Maryland got back in it behind Dixon, the Atlantic Coast Conference player of the year who finished the first half with 19 points.

The Terrapins went up 44-37 at halftime and

Kansas foward Drew Gooden (0) defends as Terps guard Steve Blake goes to the basket during the first half.

Kansas, despite getting in serious foul trouble of its own, was able to stay within striking distance.

Jeff Boschee's 3-pointer with 12:08 to play had the Jayhawks within 60-55. The Terrapins then went on a 10-0 run, the last five points coming from Holden, and it was 70-55 with 10:08 left.

The Terps went up by as many as 20 points, 83-63 on a 3 by Dixon with 6:04 to play.

Kansas, which was in the Final Four for the first time since 1993, made it exciting with the late run, but coach Roy Williams will again have to wait at least one more season for his first national championship.

Boschee, who finished 5-for-13 from 3-point range and had 17 points, got the Jayhawks within five points for the first time with a 3 with 2:04 left, making it 87-82.

Chris Wilcox blocks the shot of Drew Gooden during the first half. After Dixon's big shot from the baseline and one free throw from Blake, Boschee made it 90-85 with his last 3 with 27 seconds to play.

Gooden's 3-pointer made it 92-88 with 19 seconds left, but some of the Kansas players signaled for a timeout when the ball went through. It may not have been as dramatic as when Chris Webber made the same mistake for Michigan against North Carolina in the 1993 championship game, but it cost the Jayhawks dearly.

Dixon made the one free throw on the technical and Byron Mouton added two on the ensuing possession. Drew Nicholas capped the scoring with two free throws with .1 seconds left.

The game provided the expected offense. Kansas came in leading the nation at 91 points per game and Maryland was a couple of spots behind at 85.3.

Dixon also provided what he has throughout the tournament for the Terrapins, scoring at least 27 points for the fourth time in five games.

Looking ahead to playing Indiana, he said: "It will be a tough game. This is our year, and hopefully we come ready Monday night."

Kansas' Wayne Simien (23) and Maryland's Brett Ballard (3) scramble for a loose ball in the first half.

Kansas guard Nick Collison (4) and Lonny Baxter (35) fight for possession under the basket in first period play in the the semifinals of the Final Four in the Georgia Dome.

Kansas (88)

	min	fg m-a	ft m-a	rb o-t	a	pf	tp
Collison	33	9-14	3-4	3-10	1	3	21
Gooden	28	5-12	3-5	3-9	3	4	15
Hinrich	29	4-8	1-2	0-4	4	5	11
Miles	28	1-7	10-12	1-3	10	4	12
Boschee	38	6-16	0-0	0-3	2	3	17
Ballard	2	0-0	0-0	0-0	0	1	0
Langford	24	2-6	4-8	1-5	2	4	8
Carey	4	0-1	0-0	0-0	0	1	0
Simien	14	2-3	0-0	2-5	0	2	4
Totals	200	29-67	21-31	10-39	22	27	88

Percentages: FG .433, FT .677. **3-Point Goals:** 9-23, .391 (Boschee 5-13, Gooden 2-2, Hinrich 2-3, Langford 0-1, Miles 0-4). **Team Rebounds:** 5. **Blocked Shots:** 3 (Collison, Gooden, Simien). **Turnovers:** 16 (Hinrich 5, Boschee 4, Collison 3, Miles 3, Simien 1). **Steals:** 6 (Miles 2, Boschee 1, Collison 1, Gooden 1, Hinrich 1). **Technical Fouls:** Bench.

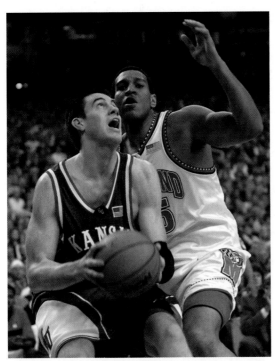

Lonny Baxter (35) tries to defend against Kansas guard Nick Collison (4).

Maryland (97)

	min	fg m-a	ft m-a	rb o-t	a	pf	tp
Mouton	29	4-9	4-4	3-6	2	2	12
Wilcox	26	8-15	2-3	3-9	1	4	18
Baxter	14	2-4	0-0	2-7	0	5	4
Dixon	37	10-18	8-11	0-3	2	2	33
Blake	32	1-7	5-9	0-3	11	4	8
Nicholas	23	2-9	2-2	0-2	2	2	7
Randle	15	1-3	0-1	1-2	0	1	2
Holden	24	4-5	5-5	2-5	0	4	13
Totals	200	32-70	26-35	11-37	18	24	97

Percentages: FG .457, FT .743. **3-Point Goals:** 7-21, .333 (Dixon 5-11, Blake 1-4, Nicholas 1-5, Holden 0-1). **Team Rebounds:** 3. **Blocked Shots:** 9 (Wilcox 4, Baxter 2, Randle 2, Holden 1). **Turnovers:** 13 (Blake 5, Baxter 2, Nicholas 2, Wilcox 2, Dixon 1, Mouton 1). **Steals:** 7 (Dixon 2, Baxter 1, Blake 1, Holden 1, Mouton 1, Wilcox 1). **Technical Fouls:** None. **Attendance:** 53,378.

Maryland's Juan Dixon, (3) and Steve Blake savor the win over the Jayhawks.

Maryland's Chris Wilcox (54) blocks a shot by Kansas' Drew Gooden (0) during the first half in the NCAA semifinal in Atlanta, Georgia.

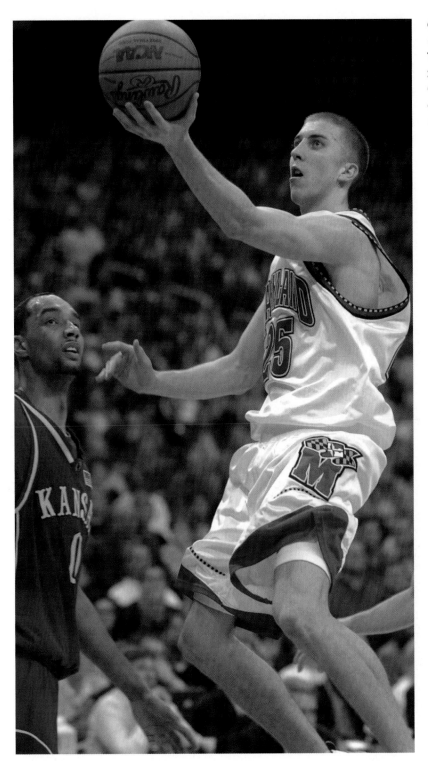

Guard Steve Blake (25) goes to the basket as Kansas forward Drew Gooden (0) looks on during the second half.

Maryland coach Gary Williams reacts on the sidelines after a mistaken play by the Terps during first period play against Kansas in the semifinals.

Kansas' Wayne Simien fails to block a shot by Chris Wilcox (54) in the first half.

Mighty Maryland!
Terps Defeat Hoosiers

Terps Prove it Has the Stuff of Champions

Juan Dixon scores 18 points in NCAA title win

By Joe Drape
The New York Times

Score by Periods	1st	2nd		Total
Indiana	25	27	—	52
Maryland	31	33	—	64

ATLANTA, April 1, 2002 — The coach was supposed to be too uptight to lead a team through six tournament games. When one senior co-captain began his collegiate career, he was thought to be too skinny, another was deemed too fat and the third unable to play defense. But after Maryland defeated Indiana tonight, 64-52, Coach Gary Williams, Juan Dixon, Lonny Baxter and Byron Mouton now wear only one label: champions.

Williams changed nothing tonight as his team grinded its way to Maryland's first national title. He stomped, bellowed and had vein-popping exchanges with his players.

A coach that sweats through up to 10 suits a season was drenched as the dead-eyed Indiana shooters kept getting loose for 3-point shots and finally took the lead, 44-42, with 10 minutes left.

But Dixon, who endured the death of his parents from AIDS-related illnesses while he was in high school, had put on 25 pounds and willed himself to become a sleek scoring machine with a knack for scoring spirit-killing baskets at opportune times. He did it again tonight, scoring 18 points, none of

Right: Guard Steve Blake (25) passes around coverage by Indiana foward Jared Jeffries (1) during second half.

Opposite page: Maryland's Lonny Baxter (35) fights for possession under the basket with Indiana foward Jared Jeffries (1) during first half.

Maryland's Juan Dixon reacts to a referee's call during second half.

them more important than a 3-pointer that triggered an 18-6 run to end the game and bury the determined Hoosiers.

Dixon, named the most valuable player of the N.C.A.A. tournament, had plenty of help from his co-captains.

Over four years, the 6-foot-8 Baxter had turned a doughboy frame into 260 pounds of muscle that hung from his wide shoulders like Sheetrock. Tonight, he walled off the middle, wore down the Hoosiers and grabbed 14 rebounds to go with 15 points.

Mouton, who was a shoot-first leading scorer at Tulane before transferring after his sophomore season, transformed himself into Maryland's defensive stopper. He scored only 4 points, but late in the game he hurtled beneath the basket and pitched a certain turnover to the backcourt to save one possession, and he came up with a critical offensive rebound moments later.

"Not many coaches get a chance to coach three great seniors like this," Williams said. "It was a thrill for me to watch these guys work this hard and get their reward."

The title game was not the prettiest played 40 minutes in the National Collegiate Athletic Association tournament. Both teams shot spottily and endured long stretches without a field goal. Fortunately for Maryland (32-4), its seven-minute drought came in the first half. Indiana, on the other hand, lost its range on 3-pointers in the final eight minutes.

"Plain and simple, they were the better team," the Hoosiers' Jeff Newton said.

Indiana (25-12) was considered the underdog despite the fact that it was seeking the sixth championship in its history and carried a title-game record of 5-0. The Hoosiers were seeded No. 5 in the South Regional when the tournament began, just two seasons removed from the divisive firing of the basketball icon Bob Knight, and were not expected to get past the pretournament favorite Duke in the Round of 16, let alone Oklahoma in the semifinals.

The Hoosiers were shooting 52 percent in the tournament from beyond the arc and 71 percent in the last two games, and showed a penchant for heating up quickly. They hit seven straight 3-pointers against Oklahoma and eight straight against Kent State.

Midway through the second half, the predominantly Indiana crowd among the 53,406 in the Georgia Dome arose, anticipating another long-range bombardment after Dane Fife hit back-to-back 3-pointers to key a 17-7 run.

When Kyle Hornsby popped in the deep left corner for another 3-pointer that fell, and Newton skyed for a tip-in to tie the score, 40-40, this cavernous arena might as well have been Assembly Hall in Bloomington, Ind. Jared Jeffries, who had been bounced around and frustrated all night by Baxter and the 6-10 Chris Wilcox, got loose for consecutive knifing layups. It was the Hoosiers 44, Maryland 42 — the only lead Indiana would have all night.

The Terps were rattled. But Dixon, as he had all tournament, refused to let Maryland lose. Fife, the Big Ten defensive player of the year, leaned, grabbed and eventually slowed Dixon for the first 12 minutes of the second half. Even though he had scored 11 points by halftime, Dixon never got anxious. First he ricocheted off a series of screens and got open on the wing for a 3-pointer to reclaim the lead for Maryland, 45-44.

"I was just trying to be patient," Dixon said. "I tried to let the game just come to me." He said he

> "It just tells you (Juan Dixon) has no fear," said of Dixon. "If you are going to win a national championship, your best player has to step up and make plays. And he did that."
>
> **— Indiana Coach Mike Davis**

Lonny Baxter (35) shoots under pressure from Indiana foward Jarrad Odle (43).

"got a great pass" from Steve Blake "and was able to knock that one down."

Then, a minute and half later, he got loose in the corner for a high, arcing 3-pointer, the one that set Maryland off and running, and provided Dixon and his fellow seniors with a crowning moment to end their collegiate careers.

"It just tells you he has no fear," Indiana Coach Mike Davis said of Dixon. "If you are going to win a national championship, your best player has to step up and make plays. And he did that."

For Maryland, the first national title is about perseverance for a coach who resurrected a scandal-riddled program in 1989, for three seniors who began their collegiate careers as projects.

"I am so proud of everyone on this team," Dixon said. "Lonny and me beat the odds and led our team to a title. Coach Williams took a chance on me and I thank him for that. We wanted to do something special."

Tonight, they did.

Indiana forward Jeff Newton (50) and Jared Jeffries (1) fight for control under the basket with Lonny Baxter (35).

Indiana (52)

	min	fg m-a	ft m-a	rb o-t	a	pf	tp
Jeffries	32	4-11	0-1	1-7	3	4	8
Hornsby	35	5-12	0-1	2-5	0	4	14
Odle	18	0-4	0-3	1-4	1	2	0
Coverdale	32	3-11	0-0	0-4	2	2	8
Fife	36	4-9	0-0	2-5	1	3	11
Moye	7	1-1	0-0	0-0	0	1	2
Leach	2	0-0	0-0	0-0	0	0	0
Perry	10	1-3	0-0	0-1	0	1	3
Newton	28	2-7	2-2	3-5	2	3	6
Totals	**200**	**20-58**	**2-7**	**9-31**	**9**	**20**	**52**

Percentages: FG .345, FT .286. **3-Point Goals:** 10-23, .435 (Hornsby 4-8, Fife 3-6, Coverdale 2-7, Perry 1-1, Jeffries 0-1). **Team Rebounds:** 1. **Blocked Shots:** 3 (Jeffries 1, Leach 1, Newton 1). **Turnovers:** 16 (Coverdale 4, Jeffries 4, Fife 2, Moye 2, Hornsby 1, Newton 1, Odle 1, Perry 1). **Steals:** 10 (Coverdale 2, Fife 2, Hornsby 2, Jeffries 1, Moye 1, Newton 1, Odle 1). **Technical Fouls:** None.

Maryland (64)

	min	fg m-a	ft m-a	rb o-t	a	pf	tp
Mouton	27	1-5	2-2	2-4	1	2	4
Wilcox	24	4-8	2-4	2-7	0	3	10
Baxter	32	6-15	3-8	2-14	0	1	15
Dixon	38	6-9	4-4	1-5	3	1	18
Blake	33	2-6	2-2	0-6	3	2	6
Nicholas	22	1-2	5-6	1-3	0	0	7
Randle	4	1-1	0-0	0-0	0	1	2
Holden	20	0-2	2-2	1-3	4	3	2
Totals	**200**	**21-48**	**20-28**	**9-42**	**11**	**13**	**64**

Percentages: FG .438, FT .714. **3-Point Goals:** 2-9, .222 (Dixon 2-4, Holden 0-1, Nicholas 0-1, Blake 0-3). **Team Rebounds:** 4. **Blocked Shots:** 6 (Baxter 3, Holden 1, Mouton 1, Wilcox 1). **Turnovers:** 16 (Dixon 7, Blake 4, Baxter 1, Holden 1, Mouton 1, Nicholas 1, Wilcox 1). **Steals:** 12 (Dixon 5, Blake 2, Mouton 2, Baxter 1, Nicholas 1, Wilcox 1). **Technical Fouls:** None. **Attendance:** 53,406.

Maryland Picks the Hoosiers' Pockets

By Thomas George
The New York Times

ATLANTA — In the national championship game, Indiana ran into a team that squeezed the Hoosiers' offense and then stomped it flat. Afterward, Indiana looked dazed, offering that wobbly look that every Indiana opponent had shown during this tournament.

Turnabout was nasty for the Hoosiers.

Maryland is not the champion because of its fancy offense. No, Maryland beat Indiana by 64-52 tonight for its first national basketball crown because of its defense.

Maryland offered one of the best defensive performances in a title game that this tournament has seen. Just ask Indiana.

"We haven't really faced a defense that could do the things they did," Indiana guard Tom Coverdale said.

Up and down the Indiana lineup, the numbers revealed that.

Indiana did not shoot well (34.5 percent), did not pass well (16 turnovers) and did not dispense the basketball efficiently (9 assists). It played a fair brand of defense against Maryland and got the kind of score that is to the Hoosiers' liking. A game with the scores in the 50's and 60's is usually an Indiana game all the way.

But look at what Maryland did. The Terrapins flipped the game plans.

"Coach told us," Maryland forward Chris Wilcox said, "in order to win this game we had to step out there and play defense. That's what we did."

They did it first by denying Indiana the passing lanes. Indiana is a team that relies on a motion-and-passing offense. Indiana got the motion right; the passing suffered badly. Led by guard Juan Dixon, Maryland clogged those passing lanes, forcing the Hoosiers into mistakes and then making them gun-shy about passes even when the lanes appeared clear.

Dixon scored a game-high 18 points, but his 5 steals were nearly as important.

"They put a lot of pressure on the ball no matter where it was, and they were in the passing lanes all night," Indiana forward Jeff Newton said. "Dixon was like a nightmare out there. We knew he was quick, but he seemed everywhere at once. And by doing that, he got into our heads a little bit and every pass seemed like it was hard to make. We fought them back, but they never quit. Tonight they were the better team."

It was a steady defensive game for Maryland. The Terps limited Indiana to 25 points in the first half and 27 in the second half.

"Their inside defense was great," Coverdale said. "They didn't have to double-team as much, so they could just lock down on our shooters."

Mike Davis, Indiana's coach, was impressed with Maryland's defensive mind-set.

"They did a great job in the passing lanes and were really chesting us up defensively," Davis said. "We weren't strong with the ball. They always kept their hands on it. When we had open looks, they were there. We couldn't take shots because the did a great job of taking away our shots."

And Maryland did it all night long.

"Our game plan had two main points, and that was to stop Jared Jeffries and contain their 3-point shooting," Maryland guard Drew Nicholas said. "We did those two things. I'm sure they are surprised to look up at the score and see how low it is and that we still won. We take pride in that. We take pride in our defense."

Maryland used fullcourt and halfcourt pressure and a variety of halfcourt traps that helped slow

Chris Wilcox (54) fights for possession with Indiana's Jared Jeffries (1).

Indiana. But it was Maryland's hard work in the paint and on the perimeter against Indiana's half-court offense that crushed the Hoosiers.

Jeffries scored only 8 points on 4 of 11 shooting. Forward Jarrad Odle was 0 for 4 from the field and did not score. Coverdale shot 3 for 11. Newton was 2 for 7. Jeffries and Coverdale each made four turnovers.

Indiana guard Dane Fife defended Dixon and then watched Dixon defend the Hoosiers.

"He is difficult from the standpoint that he is so quick," Fife said. "He got into a zone in the game on both ends, and it was tough. He's really worked hard to get where he's at, and I really respect that. I respect Maryland."

After being squeezed and pressured so tightly, after watching Maryland win a game they consider "Indiana style," all of the Hoosiers do.

The Terps celebrate after their 64-52 victory over Indiana in the NCAA Men's Final in Atlanta. The win gave Maryland its first national championship in basketball.

Guard Steve Blake (25) celebrates with Lonny Baxter.

A jubilant Juan Dixon enjoys the thrills of the post-game excitement.

Maryland coach Gary Williams swings the net — the final symbol of victory.

Gary Williams, second from left, talks to his team in the first half at the ACC Men's Basketball Tournament semifinal game against North Carolina State. The 86-82 loss to the Wolf Pack served as a wake up call for the Terrapins.

The Driving Force for Maryland

By Joe Drape
The New York Times

College Park, Md., March 28, 2002 — He stomps on the sideline, and sometimes his feet leave the floor and land with a startling thud. His arms flail as if he were a cop at an intersection trying to orchestrate traffic to heavy metal music. He glares, bellows, screams and sweats so much that each season he buys 10 new suits. Win or lose, Maryland coach Gary Williams always looks the same after a game, like a patient rolled out of surgery: exhausted, hurting and not ready for anything beyond sucking ice chips.

Williams, 56, wants to hear nothing about how he has mellowed, of how last year's trip beyond the N.C.A.A. Round of 16 for the first time in 24 years as a head coach and into the Final Four has sated or sedated him. Only his 2-year-old grandson, David, has been able to do that.

"You got to coach to your personality," Williams said in his clenched-jaw monotone voice. "I'm not afraid to tell my players some things, and they're not afraid to tell me what they think."

His players back Williams on both counts.

"He's exactly the same — if anything he is hungrier," point guard Steve Blake said.

During Maryland's 90-82 victory over Connecticut in the East Regional final, Williams yanked one of his seniors, Byron Mouton, out of the game after the Huskies' Johnnie Selvie had sliced in front of him for a rebound off a missed free throw. The coach leaned into him and roared; the player jawed right back.

"He expects you to talk back," Mouton said. "It's like a father with a son. You can't stand there and be mute or then your father won't know where your mind is at."

The minds of Williams and the Terrapins are on Kansas and a much-awaited trip to the finals. Mouton, Juan Dixon and Lonny Baxter are seniors, Blake is a junior, and all were starters on a Maryland team that lost a 22-point lead to Duke last year in the national semifinals.

The occasional sideline tiff notwithstanding, Williams and his team have demonstrated remarkable discipline in running up a 30-4 record in pursuit of Maryland's first national title. Just as Dixon and Baxter have been nearly flawless in the tournament, averaging 26 and 18.8 points, Williams has matched them on bench. To slow down UConn, Williams switched from man-to-man to a 3-2 zone defense he rarely deployed in the regular season. It worked.

In the final minute, Williams put a scoreless Blake back in the lineup, and Blake responded by drilling an off-balance 3-pointer with 25 seconds left that finally quelled the Huskies' rally. Throughout the season, Williams has recognized and corrected his team's flaws, perhaps none more vital in the tournament than its problems at the free-throw line.

Over a five-game span in November, the Terps shot 53.4 percent at the line. Williams made his players take extra shots at practice and recorded them on videotape; he and his staff spent countless hours working with each player. By season's end Maryland was a 71.4 percent free-throw-shooting team; in the tournament, it is shooting 85.7 percent (78 for 91) from the line.

Williams may dispute the notion that last year's drive to the Final Four tempered his personality, but those who know him believe the experience may have centered him.

"For the first time, Gary looks comfortable with himself," said Len Elmore, Maryland's career rebounding leader, who is a television analyst. "Maybe it is because he's taken them to the Promised Land. Maybe it is because he knows he's finally got the talent he's always wanted."

Mark Few, the Gonzaga coach, became close to Williams on the summer clinic circuit. Last year, he turned to Williams for career advice. Because of the Zags' recent success, Few, 39, was and continues to be pursued by bigger colleges; he is on the short list for the vacant job at the University of Washington.

Williams was once young and peripatetic, moving from American University to Boston College and Ohio State until 1989, when he arrived at Maryland.

the cocaine overdose of Len Bias, the academic scandal that led to the resignation of Coach Lefty Driesell and the N.C.A.A. investigation that led to the firing of Driesell's successor, Bob Wade. A year into Williams's tenure, the Terps received a two-year ban on postseason play and loss of scholarships for violations that had occurred under Wade.

Still, Williams persevered and Maryland returned to the N.C.A.A. tournament in 1994, the first of nine consecutive appearances. The dominance of its Atlantic Coast Conference rival Duke and Coach Mike Krzyzewski perhaps eclipsed this achievement. The two have been inextricably linked much like Captain Ahab and Moby Dick: Krzyzewski winning three national titles; Williams failing to get out of the Round of 16.

"Everything is always Duke, Duke, Duke," said Baxter, who was flummoxed last week when asked to comment on the Blue Devils' stunning exit from the tournament. "We're always second behind Duke. This year, they're out of the tournament and we're still advancing."

Williams is used to those queries and, in many ways, driven by that chase. Last year's semifinal lost to Duke was devastating. His grandson, David, and the child's toy cars diverted the coach's heartbreak in the immediate hours after the defeat. The two played on the floor of a Minneapolis hotel room.

"It probably took me until the first day of practice this year to get over that loss," Williams confessed.

But he took some comfort in the fact that his team was on college basketball's biggest stage and good enough to play in the second most important game of the season.

"He told me on paper that he made all the right moves, but it took its toll personally," Few said. "He got more driven; he got divorced. He told me that I better be sure of what I want from life as well as basketball. He was incredibly thoughtful."

What Williams decided he wanted was to build a program and grow old with it. He wanted to do it at his alma mater: he was the starting point guard for the Terrapins from 1965 to 1967 and their captain as a senior. The Terps were on the skids after

"I think once you've been there, you kind of have the goal, since you did it before," Williams said. "Before that seemed like an unreachable goal, almost. But once you've been there, you think: 'Wow. Maybe it's possible.'"

It is as close as Williams comes to conceding that last season began a transformation, and that there is hope for greater success.

This weekend Williams will stomp, bellow, flail, sweat and, maybe, just maybe, smile.

Dixon Puts Maryland on His Shoulders

BY JOE DRAPE
The New York Times

ATLANTA -- What does drifting along the baseline and hitting a leaner that your team absolutely needs to cut the heart out of Kansas mean when you have lost your parents to AIDS-related illnesses? What does showing that you are the best player in the country and carrying Maryland to its first national title game mean when you have had everything from your size to your SAT scores questioned and dismissed?

For Juan Dixon, it means everything and nothing at all. If Indiana is the feel-good story of this N.C.A.A. tournament, Dixon is its do-right partner. The phrase "Only the Strong Survive," which is tattooed on his right biceps, is not a hollow anthem. The names Phil and Nita etched on his left arm are motivation, as well as a memorial to his parents, Phil Jr. and Juanita, who battled drug addiction and died within 16 months of each other when he was in high school.

No matter what happens when Maryland faces Indiana on Monday night in the national championship game, Dixon has accomplished a great deal and he knows it.

"I have worked hard the last four years," he said today. "I had a dream to become a big-time college basketball player. My brother believed in me, and I believed in myself.

"I've been able to develop into the player I am today, and hopefully I'll continue to improve as a person and a player."

The team records and raves Dixon has earned throughout his senior season are evidence that an overlooked 140-pound high school player has realized his dream. Dixon, a guard, is Maryland's career leading scorer, has won more games than any previous Terrapin player (109) and has averaged 27.4 points in the tournament.

Before Maryland's semifinal against Kansas, Jayhawks Coach Roy Williams said he could not find a weakness in Dixon's game. After Dixon scored 33 against his team, Williams settled for one word: sensational.

But perhaps the player who will guard him Monday night, Indiana's Dane Fife, uttered the best testament to how Dixon's background and performance resonate. Fife is a senior who grew up in Clarkston, Mich., a long way from the projects of Dixon's native Baltimore. But Fife speaks with awe about a person he hardly knows.

"I have the utmost and amazing respect for Juan Dixon," Fife said. "What he has gone through in his life is amazing. I am not really sure why he is still playing for Maryland since I think he should be playing in the pros right now."

Dixon remains a Terp because no one ever thought he would be one and because it took him so long to get to Maryland. He was a shooter in high school with a perfect stroke honed by as many as 300 jump shots a day. But Dixon was a wispy 6 feet 3 inches with toothpick legs and was projected, at best, as a 3-point specialist off the bench.

He knew he was better than that, but first he had to take the SAT. He twice failed to achieve the minimum score required by the N.C.A.A. That prompted Dixon to take a job as a dock attendant at Baltimore's Inner Harbor when he should have been in his first semester at Maryland.

At night, he studied with his girlfriend's mother, a professor at Morgan State. When he raised his SAT score to 1060, it was deemed suspiciously high by testing administrators and the results were negated. Dixon took the test again with nearly identical results and finally enrolled at Maryland at midterm.

Juan Dixon was named the MVP of the Final Four in Atlanta.

"A lot of people counted me out," Dixon said. "Me not having my parents around, it was a little harder. But I stayed strong. I had my extended family."

That extended family includes his brother Phil, a Baltimore police officer; his grandmother Roberta Graves; and several aunts and uncles. They are here to rally around a confident, willful soul whose only quirk is obsessive cleanliness. He showers after warm-ups and suits up again before game time, and sometimes he takes plastic cutlery to restaurants.

What has distinguished Dixon's play in the tournament is his ability to take over the game when Maryland seems to be at its most vulnerable. With three minutes left in the East Regional final against Connecticut, Dixon made a 3-pointer to tie the score at 77-77 and break the spirit of the Huskies. When Kansas jumped to a 13-2 lead in Saturday's semifinal, Dixon reeled off 10 points to get the Terps back in the game.

Then in the final minutes, he stopped the Jayhawks' late rally by hitting that leaner to give Maryland a 7-point lead. Dixon is perceptive enough to know that this knack for never quitting, never being rattled, was hard won.

"I just stay strong mentally," he said. "I struggled growing up. I lost my parents at an early age. I could've folded then. But you got to stay strong. I do have an edge when I step on the court because you always got to believe in yourself, and I believe."

Now Dixon has one final game, one last opportunity as a collegian to tap his chest lightly before he shoots a free throw, as is his habit. Beneath his jersey is a tattooed likeness of his mother.

He wants to win badly the game against Indiana Monday night; he wants a successful professional basketball career. But today Dixon remained in the here and now and allowed himself to relish what he has accomplished as a basketball player, as a student, and as a person of remarkable resilience.

"I can't believe I'm in a championship game," he said, letting a smile crack his usually stoic face. "I've had a great college career. I've had a great college experience."

Date	Opponent	Site	Result	Score
Nov. 8	Arizona (Coaches vs. Cancer IKON Classic)	New York, N.Y.	Loss	71-67
Nov. 9	Temple (Consolation)	New York, N.Y.	Won	82-74
Nov. 17	American	College Park, Md.	Won	83-53
Nov. 24	Delaware State	College Park, Md.	Won	77-53
Nov. 27	Illinois (ACC/Big Ten Challenge)	College Park, Md.	Won	76-63
Dec. 2	Princeton (BB&T Classic)	Washington, D.C.	Won	61-53
Dec. 3	UConn (BB&T Classic -- Championship Game)	Washington, D.C.	Won	77-65
Dec. 9	Detroit	College Park, Md.	Won	79-54
Dec. 11	Monmouth	College Park, Md.	Won	91-55
Dec. 21	Oklahoma	Norman, Okla.	Loss	72-56
Dec. 27	William & Mary	College Park, Md.	Won	103-75
Dec. 30	NC State	Raleigh, N.C.	Won	72-65
Jan. 3	Norfolk State	College Park, Md.	Won	92-69
Jan. 9	North Carolina	College Park, Md.	Won	112-79
Jan. 13	Georgia Tech	Atlanta, Ga.	Won	92-87
Jan. 17	Duke	Durham, N.C.	Loss	99-78
Jan. 20	Clemson	College Park, Md.	Won	99-90
Jan. 23	Wake Forest	Winston-Salem, N.C.	Won	85-63
Jan. 26	Florida State	College Park, Md.	Won	84-63
Jan. 31	Virginia	Charlottesville, Va.	Won	91-87
Feb. 03	NC State	College Park, Md.	Won	89-73
Feb. 10	North Carolina	Chapel Hill, N.C.	Won	92-77
Feb. 13	Georgia Tech	College Park, Md.	Won	85-65
Feb. 17	Duke	College Park, Md.	Won	87-73
Feb. 20	Clemson	Clemson, S.C.	Won	84-68
Feb. 24	Wake Forest	College Park, Md.	Won	90-89
Feb. 27	Florida State	Tallahassee, Fla.	Won	96-63
March 3	Virginia	College Park, Md.	Won	112-92
March 8	Florida State	Charlotte, N.C.	Won	85-59
March 9	NC State (ACC Tourney)	Charlotte, N.C.	Loss	86-82
March 15	Siena (NCAA Tournament 1st Round)	Washington, D.C.	Won	85-70
March 17	Wisconsin (NCAA Second Round)	Washington, D.C.	Won	87-57
March 22	Kentucky (NCAA East Region Semifinal)	Syracuse, NY	Won	78-68
March 24	UConn (NCAA Regional Final)	Syracuse, NY	Won	90-82
March 30	Kansas (NCAA Final Four)	Atlanta, Ga.	Won	97-88
April 1	Indiana (NCAA Championship)	Atlanta, Ga.	Won	64-52